TREASURY OF LITERATURE

ALL EARS

SENIOR AUTHORS

ROGER C. FARR
DOROTHY S. STRICKLAND

AUTHORS

RICHARD F. ABRAHAMSON
ELLEN BOOTH CHURCH
BARBARA BOWEN COULTER
BERNICE E. CULLINAN
MARGARET A. GALLEGO
W. DORSEY HAMMOND
JUDITH L. IRVIN
KAREN KUTIPER
DONNA M. OGLE
TIMOTHY SHANAHAN
PATRICIA SMITH
JUNKO YOKOTA
HALLIE KAY YOPP

SENIOR CONSULTANTS

ASA G. HILLIARD III
JUDY M. WALLIS

CONSULTANTS

ALONZO A. CRIM
ROLANDO R. HINOJOSA-SMITH
LEE BENNETT HOPKINS
ROBERT J. STERNBERG

HARCOURT BRACE & COMPANY

Orlando Austin San Diego Chicago Dallas New York

ISBN 0-15-301231-5

1 2 3 4 5 6 7 8 9 10   032 97 96 95 94

Acknowledgments

For permission to reprint copyrighted material, grateful acknowledgment is made to the following sources:

Addison-Wesley Publishing Company, Inc.: "My Favorite Word" from *Oodles of Noodles* by Lucia and James L. Hymes, Jr. Text © 1964 by Lucia and James L. Hymes, Jr.

Childrens Press, Inc.: *King Midas and His Gold* by Patricia and Fredrick McKissack, illustrated by Tom Dunnington. Copyright © 1986 by Regensteiner Publishing Enterprises, Inc. Prepared under the direction of Robert Hillerich, Ph.D.

Dutton Children's Books, a division of Penguin Books USA Inc.: Illustrations by Monica Wellington from *Who Is Tapping At My Window?* by A. G. Deming. Illustrations copyright © 1988 by Monica Wellington.

Ell-Bern Publishing Company (ASCAP): "The World Is Big, The World Is Small," lyrics and music by Ella Jenkins. Lyrics and music copyright © 1966, assigned 1968 to Ella Jenkins.

HarperCollins Publishers: *Do You Want to Be My Friend?* by Eric Carle. Protected by the Berne Convention.

Little, Brown and Company: "Notice" from *One At a Time* by David McCord. Text copyright 1952 by David McCord.

Orchard Books, New York: *Potluck* by Anne Shelby, illustrated by Irene Trivas. Text copyright © 1991 by Anne Shelby; illustrations copyright © 1991 by Irene Trivas.

Marian Reiner, on behalf of Myra Cohn Livingston: "Invitation" from *Birthday Poems* by Myra Cohn Livingston. Text copyright © 1989 by Myra Cohn Livingston. Published by Holiday House. "Picture People" from *Whispers and Other Poems* by Myra Cohn Livingston. Text © 1958, renewed 1986 by Myra Cohn Livingston.

Walker Books Limited: Better Move On, Frog! by Ron Maris. © 1989 by Ron Maris.

Illustration Credits

Key: (t) top, (b) bottom, (c) center.

Table of Contents Art

Thomas Vroman Associates, Inc., 4, 5

Theme Opening Art

Sharon O'Neil, 6, 7; Kate Gorman 80, 81

Theme Wrap-up Art

Thomas Vroman Associates, Inc., 7, 81

Dear Reader,

Use your ears and eyes to let the world come in. Open a book and let the fun begin. You'll find stories, poems, and songs. You'll meet lots of children. Get to know them and they can be your friends. You might find that they care about the same things you do.

Stories, poems, and songs speak to all of us all the time. So, let's get started. Let's turn the page and meet our new friends.

Sincerely,
The Authors

CONTENTS

Theme: ALL MINE / 6

T H E M E

All Mine

Read some stories and poems about things that are yours.

C O N T E N T S

7

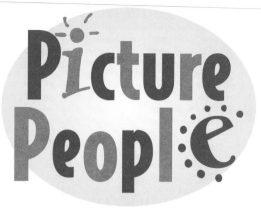

Picture People

by **Myra Cohn Livingston**

illustrated by **Mike Reed**

I like to peek
 inside a book
 where all the picture people look.

I like to peek
 at them and see
 if they are peeking back at me.

BY ERIC CARLE

11

16

24

28

33

37

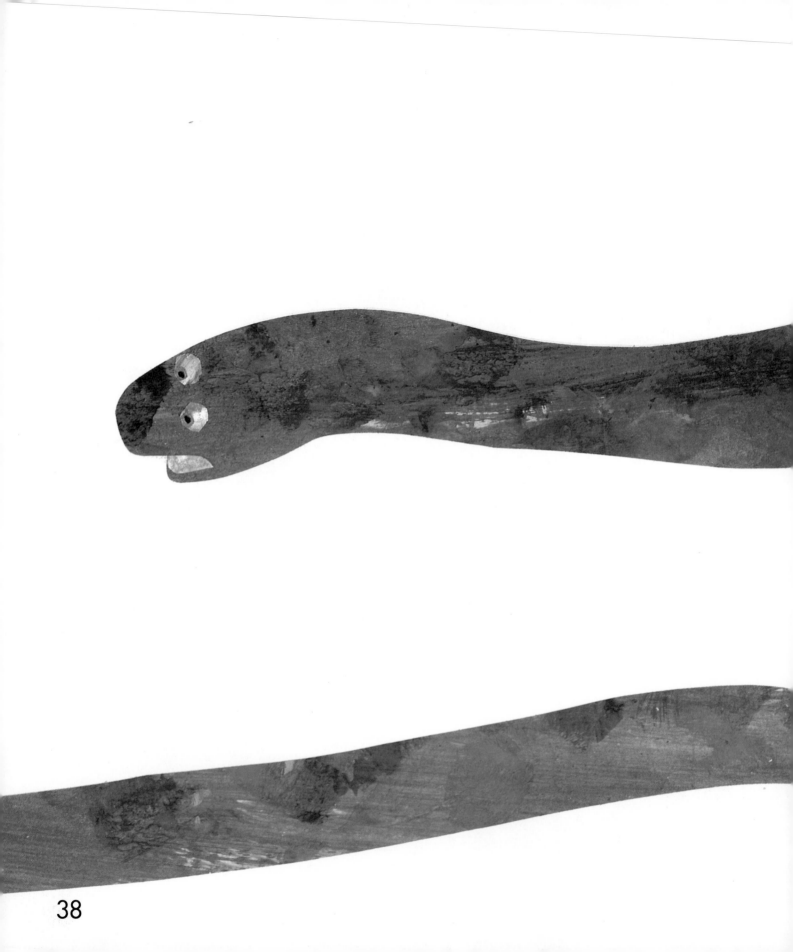

THE
VERY NICEST
PLACE

Author Unknown
illustrated by Carolyn Croll

The fish lives in the brook,
The bird lives in the tree,
But home's the very nicest place
For a little child like me.

41

P·O·T·L·U·C·K

• BY ANNE SHELBY • PICTURES BY IRENE TRIVAS •

Alpha and Betty
decided to have a potluck. So—

they called up
their friends,

cleaned up their house,

42

and set their table—
for thirty-one.

Finally . . .

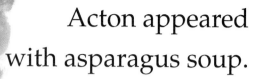

Acton appeared
with asparagus soup.

Ben brought bagels.

Christine
came
with
carrot cake
and
corn
on
the cob.

Don did dumplings.

Edmund entered with enchiladas,

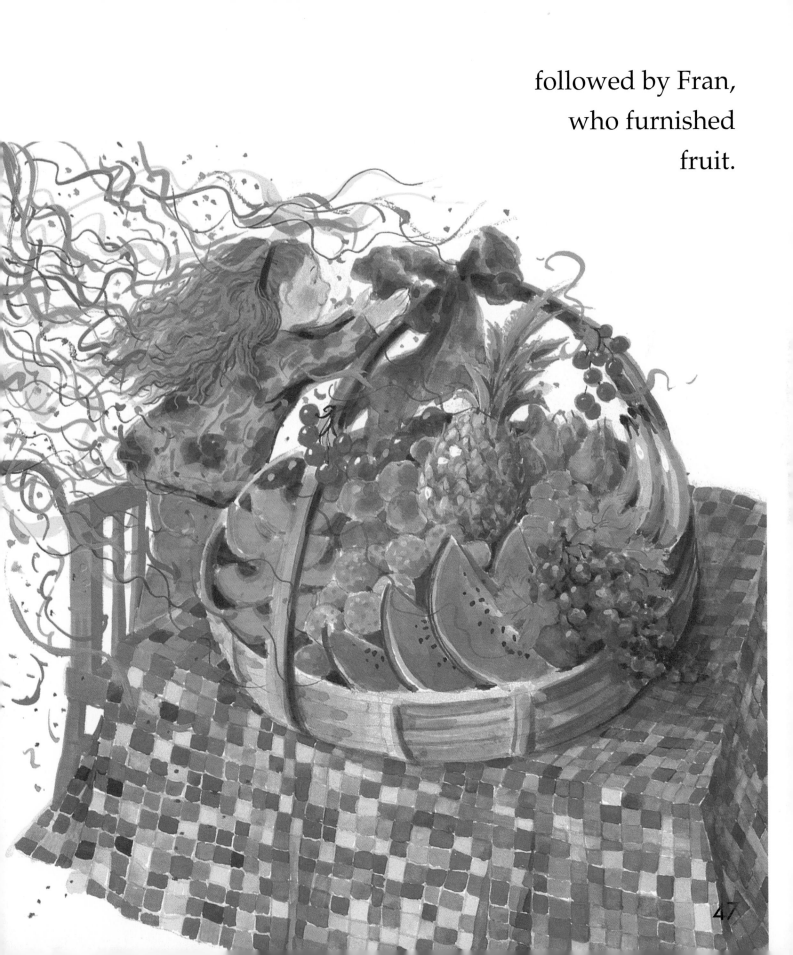

followed by Fran,
who furnished
fruit.

47

Graham had gone by Garbanzo's Bakery

to get good garlic bread.

H.B. had made
honey-sweetened hot tea.

Irene insisted on iced.

June joined in
with jelly rolls;

Kim with
a kettle of kale.

Lonnie loves lasagna,
so he brought lots of that.

Monica made mounds and mounds of mashed potatoes.

Norman knew
that oodles of noodles
would be needed.

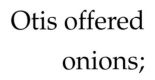

Otis offered onions;

Priscilla, a peanut-butter pie.

Quincy, of course,
brought quiche;

Rose,
her famous
rice and raisin
recipe.

Sam showed up with spaghetti sauce
subtly seasoned with spices.

The triplets turned up
with tacos;

Ursula, with
upside-down cake.

Victor ventured
vegetarian stew,

while
Wally
wowed
the crowd
with his
wonderful
waffles.

56

Xavier
brought
some
excellent
examples
of
extra-special
X-shaped
cookies.

Yolanda
said yes
to yams
and yogurt.

But somebody was missing.
Who?

Then, at the last minute . . .

Zeke and Zelda
zoomed in
with zucchini
casserole.

So they all sat down
and ate
and ate and ate
and ate and ate.

58

They ate everything

from A to Z.

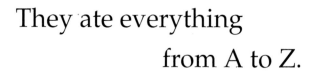

Invitation

by *Myra Cohn Livingston*
illustrated by *Mary Lynn Blasutta*

My birthday invitation
has balloons
of red and blue.

It says *come soon*
and *please reply,*

My name is on it too.

It tells the place where we will meet
And shows the time and date.

So please *reply*
And say you'll *come*

to help me celebrate!

KING MIDAS AND HIS GOLD

by
Patricia and
Fredrick McKissack

Midas was a king.
But he was not happy.
"I wish for gold," he said.
"Gold will make me happy."

Ping! He got his wish.

King Midas saw
an apple.
Ping!
It was gold.

A cup.
Ping!
It was gold.

A box.
Ping!
It was gold, too.

King Midas
was happy.
He had gold,
gold, gold.

King Midas saw
a rose.
"Oh, pretty rose."
Ping!

The rose was gold.
King Midas did not
like that.

King Midas saw his dog.
"Oh, good dog."

Ping!
The dog was gold.
King Midas did not
like that.

King Midas was king.
But he was not very happy.
He could not eat.

He could not sleep.

He could not do much.
Ping! Ping! Ping!

Ping!
The cook was gold.

Ping!
The queen was gold.

"No. No.
Go. Go.
Oh, no!"

Ping!
The princess was gold!

73

All he had was gold, gold, gold!
King Midas did not like that.

"I wish there was no
more gold," he said.
And he got his wish.

Ping!
Back came the princess,
the queen,
the cook,
the dog,

the rose,
the box,
the cup,
and the apple!

77

King Midas could eat.
He could sleep.

"No more gold," he said.
And this made
him happy.

My Favorite WORD

There is one word —
My favorite —
The very, very best.
It isn't No or Maybe.
It's Yes, Yes, Yes, *Yes*, YES!

"Yes, yes, you may," and
"Yes, of course," and
"Yes, please help yourself."
And when I want a piece of cake,
"Why, yes. It's on the shelf."

Some candy? "Yes."
A cookie? "Yes."
A movie? "Yes, we'll go."

I love it when they say my word:
Yes, *Yes*, YES! *(Not No.)*

by **Lucia and James L. Hymes, Jr.**
illustrated by **Jennie Oppenheimer**

79

THEME

A Place for Everyone

We live in a big world. There is room for everyone if we all care for each other.

CONTENTS

81

Better move on, Frog!

by Ron Maris

SHARED READING

Holes! Lots of holes!
Which one shall I have?

82

Better move on, Frog.
This hole is full of badgers.

Better move on, Frog.
This hole is full of rabbits.

Better move on, Frog.
This hole is full of owls.

Better move on, Frog.
This hole is full of mice.

Better move on, Frog.
This hole is full of bees.

But look!

Better move in, Frog.
And wait for the hole to fill up . . .

. . . like all the other holes.

NOTICE

I have a dog,
I have a cat.
I've got a frog
Inside my hat.

by David McCord
illustrated by
Ken Bowser

AWARD-WINNING
POET

111

Who Is Tapping At My Window?

by A. G. DEMING

pictures by
MONICA WELLINGTON

Who is tapping at my window?

"It's not I," said the cat.

"It's not I," said the rat.

"It's not I," said the wren.

"It's not I," said the hen.

"It's not I,"
said the
fox.

"It's not I,"
said the
ox.

"It's not I," said the loon.

"It's not I," said the raccoon.

"It's not I,"
said the
cony.

"It's not I,"
said the
pony.

"It's not I,"
said the
dog.

"It's not I,"
said the
frog.

"It's not I,"
said the
bear.

"It's not I,"
said the
hare.

Who is tapping at my window?

"It is I," said the rain,

"tapping at your windowpane."

What Shall We Do

What shall we do when we all go out,
All go out, all go out,
What shall we do when we all go out,
When we all go out to play?

When We All Go Out?

illustrated by Bernard Most

We can run in a zigzag line,
A zigzag line, a zigzag line,
We can run in a zigzag line
When we all go out to play.

THE WORLD IS
BIG
THE WORLD IS
small

By Ella Jenkins

illustrated by Kate Brennan Hall

Oh, the world is big,
And the world is small,
So there's lots of room
For the short and tall.

Oh, the world is far
And the world is wide,
But there are many different ways
To see the other side.

You can travel on a boat.
You can travel on a van.

You can travel on a jet.
You can travel on a train.

The End

You can travel in a song.
You can travel in a book.